# Buckingham Palace

## The Official Residence of England's Royal Family

**Joy Gregory**

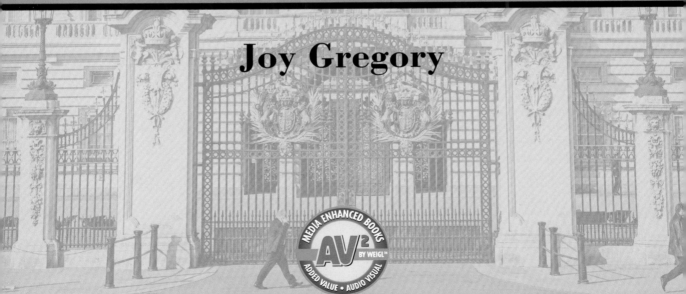

www.av2books.com

AV² provides enriched content that supplements and complements this book. Weigl's AV² books strive to create inspired learning and engage young minds in a total learning experience.

## Your AV² Media Enhanced books come alive with...

**Audio**
Listen to sections of the book read aloud.

**Key Words**
Study vocabulary, and complete a matching word activity.

**Video**
Watch informative video clips.

**Quizzes**
Test your knowledge.

**Embedded Weblinks**
Gain additional information for research.

**Slide Show**
View images and captions, and prepare a presentation.

**Try This!**
Complete activities and hands-on experiments.

**... and much, much more!**

Go to **www.av2books.com**, and enter this book's unique code.

## BOOK CODE

**H985577**

**AV² by Weigl** brings you media enhanced books that support active learning.

Published by AV² by Weigl
350 5th Avenue, 59th Floor
New York, NY 10118
Websites: www.av2books.com  www.weigl.com

Library of Congress Cataloging-in-Publication Data
Gregory, Joy (Joy Marie)
  Buckingham Palace / Joy Gregory.
     pages cm. -- (Castles of the World)
  Includes bibliographical references and index.
  ISBN 978-1-4896-3392-7 (hard cover : alk. paper) -- ISBN 978-1-4896-3393-4 (soft cover : alk. paper) -- ISBN 978-1-4896-3394-1 (single user ebk) -- ISBN 978-1-4896-3395-8 (multi-user ebk)
  1. Buckingham Palace (London, England)--Juvenile literature. 2. Great Britain--Kings and rulers--Dwellings--Juvenile literature. 3. London (England)--Buildings, structures, etc.--Juvenile literature. I. Title.
  DA687.B9G74 2015
  942.1'32--dc23
                    2015001368

Printed in the United States of America in Brainerd, Minnesota
1 2 3 4 5 6 7 8 9 0 19 18 17 16 15

032015
WEP070315

Editor: Heather Kissock
Design: Mandy Christiansen

Every reasonable effort has been made to trace ownership and to obtain permission to reprint copyright material. The publishers would be pleased to have any errors or omissions brought to their attention so that they may be corrected in subsequent printings. Weigl acknowledges Getty Images, Alamy, Corbis, iStock, Newscom, Wikipedia, and Dreamstime as its primary image suppliers for this title.

# Contents

# What Is Buckingham Palace?

Located in London, England, Buckingham Palace is an official residence of Queen Elizabeth II, the queen of the United Kingdom. The palace serves as both a home and an office for the royal family. The queen lives there when she is in London, and her **administrative** staff work there year-round. It is also where many important royal events, such as grand balls, formal dinners, and wedding receptions, are held. The palace has many types of rooms, ranging from lavish **salons** to simple office spaces, to host the variety of activities that take place there.

Buckingham Palace has been the official London residence of the British monarch since 1837.

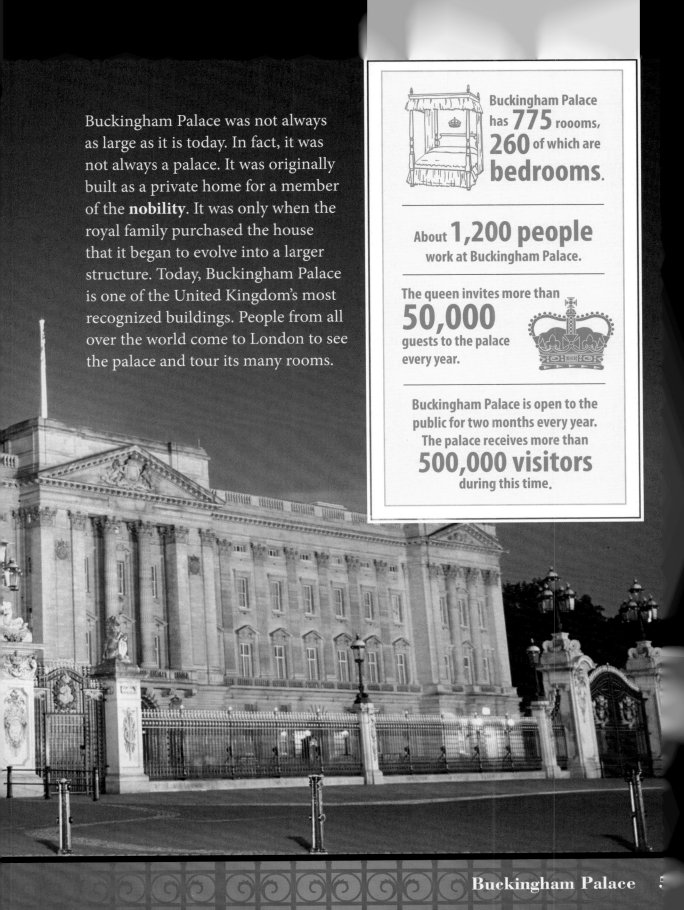

Buckingham Palace was not always as large as it is today. In fact, it was not always a palace. It was originally built as a private home for a member of the **nobility**. It was only when the royal family purchased the house that it began to evolve into a larger structure. Today, Buckingham Palace is one of the United Kingdom's most recognized buildings. People from all over the world come to London to see the palace and tour its many rooms.

Buckingham Palace has **775** roooms, **260** of which are **bedrooms**.

About **1,200 people** work at Buckingham Palace.

The queen invites more than **50,000** guests to the palace every year.

Buckingham Palace is open to the public for two months every year. The palace receives more than **500,000 visitors** during this time.

# A Step Back in Time

The first house to stand on the current site of Buckingham Palace was built in the 1600s. When the Duke of Buckingham acquired the house in 1705, he decided to demolish it and build his own. The duke and his descendants lived in Buckingham House until 1761, when it was bought by King George III and used as a private residence. Following the king's death in 1820, his son, King George IV, decided to enlarge the house. Under the supervision of **architect** John Nash, Buckingham House was transformed into a U-shaped palace. Over the years, other architects were hired to rework and add on to the palace until it became the structure that exists today.

King George III ruled the United Kingdom from 1760 to 1820.

**1705** John Sheffield, the Duke of Buckingham, builds a private residence that comes to be known as Buckingham House.

**1826** King George IV launches a plan to turn Buckingham House into a palace.

**1700**　　　**1750**　　　**1800**　　　**1840**

**1761** King George III buys Buckingham House for his family.

**1833–1834** The palace's State Rooms, where official functions are held, are completed.

**1847** At Queen Victoria's request, a new wing is added to the east end of the palace. This wing closes the open end of the building and becomes the palace's **façade**.

The original Buckingham House was designed by architect William Winde. It featured a large central block flanked by two smaller wings.

**2002** The Queen's Gallery re-opens its art exhibition after a major expansion. The gallery, which opened in 1962, is located in a chapel that was bombed during World War II.

**1913** Workers begin to remove and replace the palace's façade with new stonework.

1850      1900      1950      2010

**1852** The palace's Ball and Concert Room and Ball Supper Room are completed.

**1911** A **forecourt** is built in front of the east wing. Today, this is where a ceremony called the Changing of the Guard takes place.

**1994–1995** A new heat and power plant at Buckingham Palace starts to generate electricity for the palace.

# Buckingham Palace's Location

As when it was first built, Buckingham Palace stands in the middle of parkland. The building faces toward the Mall, a tree-lined road that leads to central London. St. James's Park runs along the south side of the road, while Green Park lies on the north side. Hyde Park, London's largest park, is located to the northwest of the palace. The area behind the palace is more developed, with shops, hotels, and office buildings just across the street.

**FLOOR SPACE** The interior floor plan of Buckingham Palace, from the basement to the top level, covers 92,000 square yards (77,000 square meters).

Buckingham Palace is located in a part of London called Westminster. Westminster is a city in its own right and has its own municipal government.

The palace is located near several British landmarks. Kensington Palace sits at the west end of Hyde Park, while St. James's Palace can be seen from the Mall. At the end of the Mall is Trafalgar Square, which pays tribute to an important British battle. The National Gallery stands on the north side of the square. It houses some of the world's best-known artworks. Westminster Abbey, where the queen was crowned, is just a short walk away. The Palace of Westminster, better known as the British Houses of Parliament, is located across from the abbey.

**GARDENS** Buckingham Palace's gardens cover 40 acres (16 hectares).

**LENGTH AND WIDTH** Buckingham Palace is 354 feet (108 m) long and 394 feet (120 m) wide.

**HEIGHT** At its highest point, the palace is 79 feet (24 meters) high.

# Outside the Palace

*Buckingham Palace is one of London's main tourist attractions. Even when people cannot go into the palace itself, there are still ways for them to get a glimpse into the royal lifestyle.*

**EAST FRONT** Also known as the façade, the East Front is the most recognizable part of Buckingham Palace. The façade has several features that allow the royal family to connect with the public. On ceremonial days, the royal family will appear on the façade's balcony to wave to the crowds. Royal carriages leave the palace through the arches along the bottom of the wall. If people want to know if the queen is at home, they can look to the top of the façade's main **pediment**. If the **royal standard** is flying on the mast, the queen is in residence.

**ROYAL MEWS** The Royal Mews, or stable, is located behind the palace. Visitors to the mews can learn about the various modes of transportation used by the royal family. The complex is home to about 30 horses and is also the storage facility for the carriages used by the royal family on formal occasions. Their fleet of cars and other motor vehicles is also on display.

**GARDENS** The palace gardens stretch out from the southwest end of the palace. The queen and her family host garden parties here throughout the summer. These immaculately groomed gardens include a variety of trees, a lake, and a small summer house, as well as more modern conveniences, such as a tennis court and a helicopter landing pad.

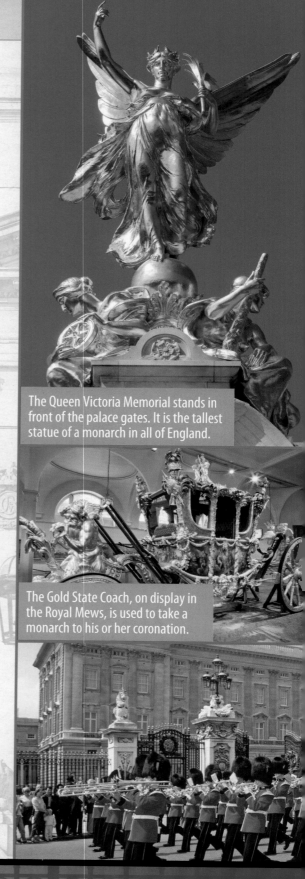

The Queen Victoria Memorial stands in front of the palace gates. It is the tallest statue of a monarch in all of England.

The Gold State Coach, on display in the Royal Mews, is used to take a monarch to his or her coronation.

When the palace opens in the summer, visitors have a chance to see the gardens at the end of their tour.

The central gate to Buckingham Palace is used only on official or ceremonial occasions.

The royal family gathers on the palace balcony following important ceremonies to acknowledge the public's good wishes.

The Changing of the Guard ceremony takes place in front of Buckingham Palace every day during the busy tourist season from May to July.

A flag always flies at the palace. If the queen is not at the palace, the **Union Jack is flown**. This is the flag of the United Kingdom.

The royal gardens are home to about **350** different types of wildflowers and **30 species** of birds.

The palace has **760** windows.

The Queen Victoria Memorial is nearly **82 feet** (25 m) high.

King George III bought Buckingham House for about **$42,000**, or **$6 million** by today's standards.

During World War II, Buckingham Palace was hit by bombs **9 times**.

Approximately **27,000** cups of tea are served at one of the queen's garden parties.

# Inside the Palace

*Buckingham Palace has a set of rooms that have been designed specifically for public functions. These State Rooms are where the queen and members of the royal family meet with invited guests.*

**THRONE ROOM** With its red and gold decor, high ceilings, and shimmering chandeliers, the Throne Room is one of Buckingham Palace's most formal rooms. It is here that **investitures** and other formal ceremonies take place. The queen's throne, or chair, sits on a **dais** at the far end of the room. A second chair beside the throne is for the queen's husband. Above the dais is a **proscenium** arch held up by two angels.

**BALLROOM** The Ballroom is the largest room in the palace. Built during Queen Victoria's reign, it opened in 1856. Approximately 120 feet (37 m) long and 59 feet (18 m) wide, it used to be the largest room in London. The Ballroom is used for state dinners. These are functions held when government leaders from other countries visit the queen. The Ballroom is also used for concerts, royal wedding receptions, and awards ceremonies.

**PICTURE GALLERY** The queen's art collection is displayed on a rotating basis in the palace's Picture Gallery. The gallery is a 154-foot (47-m) long room that features a glass skylight ceiling. Paintings hang on the walls, and decorative art lines the length of the room. The gallery is sometimes used for receptions and small dinners. It is also where people gather before entering the Ballroom.

Portraits of past British monarchs hang on the walls of the State Dining Room.

During Queen Victoria's reign, the Throne Room also served as a ballroom.

Members of the royal family often gather in the White Drawing Room before official functions.

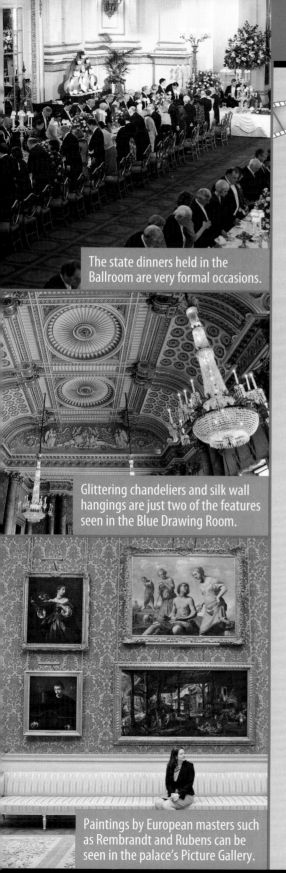

The state dinners held in the Ballroom are very formal occasions.

Glittering chandeliers and silk wall hangings are just two of the features seen in the Blue Drawing Room.

Paintings by European masters such as Rembrandt and Rubens can be seen in the palace's Picture Gallery.

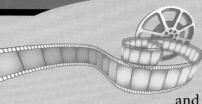

The palace has its own **post office, movie theater,** and **doctor's office.**

**Buckingham Palace has 19 State Rooms.**

**The palace has more than**

**350** clocks and watches to help the royal family stay on schedule.

The ceiling in the Ballroom is **44 feet** (13.4 m) high. That is more than **4x higher** than the ceiling in most family homes.

The palace kitchen is equipped to serve a sit-down meal to **600 people.**

**The palace's light fixtures hold more than 40,000 light bulbs.**

Buckingham Palace has **78** restrooms.

# Buckingham Palace's Builders

From a grand townhouse to a palace fit for a queen, Buckingham Palace has evolved over time. Throughout the past 300 years, many people have contributed to creating the palace that exists today. The construction of the palace required the skills of a wide range of people.

### John Nash Architect

In the 1820s, King George IV hired architect John Nash to turn Buckingham House into a palace. Nash had already been responsible for designing several sites in London, including Regent's Park and Trafalgar Square. His concept for the new palace was to expand upon the building that was already there. Nash designed the initial U-shaped palace by adding onto the building's existing wings. With the king's approval, construction soon began. However, Nash later faced criticism for spending too much money on the palace. He was dismissed from his position before the palace was completed. Nash left the profession shortly after.

Nash spent five years working on Buckingham Palace. Today, all that remains of his work is the palace's west wing.

### Edward Blore Architect

Edward Blore was hired to re-organize the palace for Queen Victoria in 1832. Prior to this project, Blore had been primarily known for designing country homes for members of the nobility. At Buckingham Palace, Blore was charged with creating more space for the queen and her family. Under Blore's supervision, construction of a new wing, the East Front, was finished in 1850. Blore left his architecture practice shortly after, but he continued to draw plans for new projects. Blore died in London in 1879.

Edward Blore also worked on projects at other royal residences, including Windsor Castle and Hampton Court Palace.

### Aston Webb Architect

When Edward Blore's East Front began to deteriorate, Sir Aston Webb was hired to create a new façade for the palace. It is this façade that is on view today. Webb was a highly respected architect. Before receiving the job at Buckingham Palace, he had already designed London's Victoria and Albert Museum, the Royal College of Science, and the Britannia Royal Naval College. He had also been knighted by Queen Victoria. His illustrious career came to an end in 1930 when he died due to injuries from a car accident.

Aston Webb was president of the Royal Institute of British Architects from 1902 to 1904.

## Architects

An architect is a person who designs and plans buildings, and then supervises their construction. Architects have to consider a number of factors. They have to understand the purpose of a building and how it will be used. This information allows them to design rooms and other spaces. To ensure that they create a building that is structurally sound, architects also have to understand construction techniques and building materials. The architects who worked on Buckingham Palace trained for many years to understand the principles behind constructing buildings.

Architects create technical drawings of the structure to be built. These drawings are consulted at all stages of the construction process.

## Quarry Workers

The stone used to rebuild Buckingham Palace's façade came from a small island in the English Channel. Preparing the stone for transport to London was the job of **quarry** workers. These people cut the stone from the rock quarry walls using chisels and hammers. They then shaped the stone into blocks using the same tools. The blocks were loaded onto a train and transported to a waiting barge, which carried the stone across the channel to London.

Today's quarry workers use drills and explosives to break up rock.

Interior designers review samples of various materials to determine which will work best in the rooms they are decorating.

## Interior Designers

Interior designers plan how a room should look. They use color, lighting, furniture, and artwork to make each room look special. In Buckingham Palace, the interior designer played a key role in planning the decorative features of the rooms. This included designing carpet patterns as well as the engravings for the palace's staircase railings and the palace's chandeliers. The designer then supervised the manufacturing process for each piece. Being an interior designer requires imagination and creativity, as well as strong organizational skills.

# Building Buckingham Palace

Buckingham Palace was planned as a showcase for the British royal family. However, its construction also had to stay within a budget. The architects had to develop creative solutions to compromise the expectation of grandeur with the reality of limited funds. Sometimes, these solutions had to be revisited. Other ideas were more successful and gave the palace the regal appearance its purpose demanded.

**THE RIGHT ROCK** When Edward Blore built the East Front, he chose to use a soft rock from France called Caen stone. Within a few years, it became apparent that the rock was disintegrating due to the moist London air. The decision was made to reface the East Front with a sturdier type of rock. The rock selected by Aston Webb was Portland stone, a type of limestone. Many of London's historic buildings are made of Portland stone. Builders like it because it can be easily cut into shape, but is still durable and able to withstand wear. Portland stone is also admired by designers for its creamy white color.

**THE GOLD STANDARD** Buckingham Palace originally had a marble arch as its main entrance. The arch had to be moved when the East Front was built. It was replaced with a gold-tipped **wrought iron** fence. Gold was a popular decorative feature at the time because it indicated wealth. As one of the most **malleable** metals, gold is also easy to mold into shape. Gold is long-lasting and does not **corrode** or break down like other metals. This makes it suitable for outdoor settings. Gold can withstand all kinds of conditions, including wind, rain, snow, and sunlight, without being degraded.

**COST SAVINGS** Even though John Nash went over budget on his renovation of Buckingham Palace, some of the choices he made during the construction showed an attempt to save money. To avoid the need to constantly clean chimneys, he opted to use glazed bricks and designed the chimneys to avoid the sharp corner angles where soot typically gathers. Nash also substituted wood for marble when creating some of the palace's decorative features. Using a technique called scagliola, he had plaster applied to a wood base and then painted the plaster to look like the expensive stone. This technique was used on columns throughout the interior of the palace.

Today, visitors to Buckingham Palace can still see Aston Webb's Portland stone façade on the East Front.

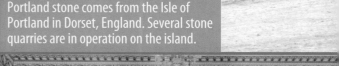

Portland stone comes from the Isle of Portland in Dorset, England. Several stone quarries are in operation on the island.

When gold plating is attached to an object, such as a fence railing, the object is said to be gilded.

The columns in Buckingham Palace's Music Room have been created using the scagliola technique.

# Similar Palaces around the World

Buckingham Palace is neoclassical in design. This architectural style is influenced by the buildings of ancient Greece and Rome. Common features in neoclassical buildings include columns, pediments, and domes. Neoclassical style was an architectural trend throughout the 18th and 19th centuries. During that time, a number of castles and palaces were built in this style.

## Culzean Castle

**BUILT:** 1777–1792, 1877–1878 AD
**LOCATION:** Ayrshire, Scotland
**DESIGN:** Robert Adam, Wardrop & Reid
**DESCRIPTION:** Like Buckingham Palace, Culzean Castle began as a smaller building. Home to members of the Scottish nobility, it underwent a dramatic renovation in the 1700s and was further improved in the late 1800s. The castle sits at the crest of a cliff, looking over the valley below. Its architecture is known for its simplicity and **symmetry**, with features repeated to provide balance to the structure's appearance. The castle's interior is noted for its use of columns and its domed **cupola**.

A series of terraced gardens sit below Culzean Castle. They were added to the palace grounds in the 17th century.

# Ajuda National Palace

**BUILT:** 1802–1910 AD
**LOCATION:** Lisbon, Portugal
**DESIGN:** Francisco Xavier Fabri, José da Costa e Silva
**DESCRIPTION:** Initially planned to be built in the **Baroque** style, the Ajuda National Palace became a neoclassical structure on the orders of Portugal's King José I. The building was never completed, but was opened as a museum in the 1960s. The exterior of the building features a simple façade with a columned entrance. A series of sculptures lines the palace's lobby. Each sculpture represents a different virtue, such as generosity. The interior of the palace is decorated with grand chandeliers, lush tapestries, and **frescoed** ceilings.

The Ajuda National Palace was originally planned as a summer residence for Portugal's royal family.

# Royal Palace of Caserta

**BUILT:** 1752–1920 AD
**LOCATION:** Caserta, Italy
**DESIGN:** Luigi Vanvitelli, Carlo Vanvitelli
**DESCRIPTION:** Built for the kings of Naples, the Royal Palace of Caserta is a rectangular building in the neoclassical style. The palace covers approximately 505,904 square feet (47,000 sq. m) and is five stories high. It has two façades. One faces the forecourt, while the other looks toward the palace's gardens. The gardens are elaborate and feature a series of fountains and waterfalls. Inside, the palace has sculptures, frescoes, and a grand staircase. Like the Ajuda National Palace, the Royal Palace of Caserta remains incomplete, but is open to visitors as a museum.

The Royal Palace of Caserta was recognized for its historical and cultural value in 1997 when it was named a UNESCO World Heritage Site.

# Issues Facing the Palace

Buckingham Palace has served the United Kingdom's royal family for almost 200 years, and it is beginning to show its age. The structure is gradually deteriorating due to long-term use and exposure to a harsh environment. Due to the high cost of repairs, restoration attempts have been slow, contributing to further structural damage.

## WHAT IS THE ISSUE?

The palace exterior is exposed to harsh environmental conditions, including wind, rain, snow, and pollution.

Many of the electrical and mechanical services in the palace were installed with potentially hazardous materials during the 1940s.

## EFFECTS

Stonework is becoming loose and crumbling. Pieces have become detached and fallen to the ground.

Asbestos, a building material used to insulate the palace's electrical wiring ducts, is known to cause health problems such as lung cancer.

## ACTION TAKEN

Scaffolding was erected in at-risk areas to hold unstable stone in place. Parts of the building's façade have been refinished with a more durable type of limestone.

Work began in 2012 to strip the asbestos from the wiring ducts. Duct covers were replaced and excess wiring was removed to allow easier access for future improvements.

# Create a Gilded Crown

Gilding was one of the ways Buckingham Palace designers used artistic detail to demonstrate the wealth and status of the royal family. While gold was the preferred material for gilding at the palace, other metals can also be used to gild items. Follow the instructions below to design a royal crown gilded in silver.

## Materials
- White glue
- Pencil
- Cardboard
- Aluminum foil
- Plastic jewels, buttons, and beads
- Paper towel (optional)

## Instructions

1. Using the internet and books from the library, study some pictures of crowns worn by today's royal family and royalty from the past. Decide which features you would like to have on your crown.

2. Take the piece of cardboard, and draw an outline of the crown you would wear.

3. Trace this outline with white glue, and then use the glue to trace the crown's details. If you want to include jewels, trace around the places where you want the jewels to sit. Leave the center of the jewelled space free of glue so you can "set" a jewel inside.

4. Let the glue dry completely.

5. Carefully cover the surface of your drawing with the aluminum foil. Smooth the foil over the beaded glue. If you left areas for jewels, press the foil into the inside of those areas.

6. Once you have gilded your crown, glue your jewels onto it. Hang your completed design on your wall or the bulletin board in your classroom.

# Buckingham Palace Quiz

**Q** Which architectural style was used to design the palace?

**A** Neoclassical

**Q** Who did King George IV hire to turn Buckingham House into a palace?

**A** John Nash

**Q** What type of stone was used to reface the East Front?

**A** Portland stone

**Q** How many people tour Buckingham Palace every summer?

**A** More than 500,000

# Key Words

**administrative:** related to the running of an institution

**architect:** a person who designs buildings

**Baroque:** a type of architecture known for its ornate decoration

**corrode:** to wear away gradually

**cupola:** a small dome adorning a roof or ceiling

**dais:** a low platform

**façade:** the principal front of a building

**forecourt:** an open area in front of a building

**frescoed:** painted onto plaster

**investitures:** ceremonies in which people are given a new status or honor

**malleable:** having the ability to be stretched or bent into different shapes

**nobility:** a social class of people who have more privileges than others

**pediment:** a triangular section on the front of a building

**proscenium:** the arch that separates a stage from the auditorium

**quarry:** a pit from which stone is obtained

**royal standard:** a flag that represents the authority of a monarch

**salons:** reception rooms in large houses

**symmetry:** in balance, with each side reflecting the other

**wrought iron:** a form of iron that is tough but easy to shape

# Index

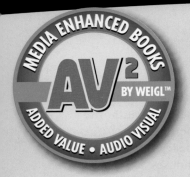

# Log on to www.av2books.com

AV² by Weigl brings you media enhanced books that support active learning. Go to www.av2books.com, and enter the special code found on page 2 of this book. You will gain access to enriched and enhanced content that supplements and complements this book. Content includes video, audio, weblinks, quizzes, a slide show, and activities.

## AV² Online Navigation

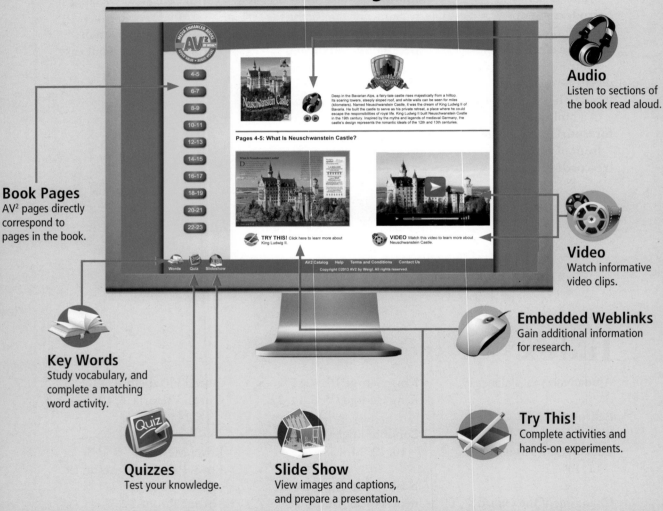

**Book Pages**
AV² pages directly correspond to pages in the book.

**Key Words**
Study vocabulary, and complete a matching word activity.

**Quizzes**
Test your knowledge.

**Slide Show**
View images and captions, and prepare a presentation.

**Audio**
Listen to sections of the book read aloud.

**Video**
Watch informative video clips.

**Embedded Weblinks**
Gain additional information for research.

**Try This!**
Complete activities and hands-on experiments.

AV² was built to bridge the gap between print and digital. We encourage you to tell us what you like and what you want to see in the future.

## Sign up to be an AV² Ambassador at www.av2books.com/ambassador.

Due to the dynamic nature of the Internet, some of the URLs and activities provided as part of AV² by Weigl may have changed or ceased to exist. AV² by Weigl accepts no responsibility for any such changes. All media enhanced books are regularly monitored to update addresses and sites in a timely manner. Contact AV² by Weigl at 1-866-649-3445 or av2books@weigl.com with any questions, comments, or feedback.